THE ARTS OF THE SIKH KINGDOMS

THE CANADIAN COLLECTIONS

ਸਿੱਖ ਰਾਜ ਘਰਾਣਿਆਂ ਦੀਆਂ ਕਲਾਵਾਂ - ਕਨੇਡੀਅਨ ਸੰਗ੍ਰਹਿ

THE ARTS OF THE SIKH KINGDOMS

THE CANADIAN COLLECTIONS

ਸਿੱਖ ਰਾਜ ਘਰਾਣਿਆਂ ਦੀਆਂ ਕਲਾਵਾਂ - ਕਨੇਡੀਅਨ ਸੰਗ੍ਰਹਿ

SEEMA BHARADIA

The Arts of the Sikh Kingdoms:
The Canadian Collections

First published in 2000 by

The Royal Ontario Museum
100 Queen's Park
Toronto, Ontario
M5S 2C6

Canadian Cataloguing-in-Publication Data

Bharadia, Seema, 1966-
The arts of the Sikh kingdoms : the Canadian collections

Catalogue of Canadian Sikh artifacts added to the exhibition, The arts of the Sikh kingdoms, held at the Royal Ontario Museum, May 22/Aug. 20, 2000.
Includes bibliographical references.
ISBN 0-88854-433-2(bound) ISBN 0-88854-434-0(pbk.)

1. Art, Sikh — Exhibitions. I. Royal Ontario Museum. II Title.

N8199.S543T67 2000 704'.2946'074713541 C00-931730-9

Editorial: Andrea Gallagher Ellis
Design: Tara Winterhalt
Production: Virginia Morin
Photography: Brian Boyle

The Royal Ontario Museum is an agency of the Ontario Ministry of Citizenship, Culture and Recreation.

Printed and bound in Canada by St. Joseph's/M.O.M. Printing

The Royal Ontario Museum gratefully acknowledges the generous support of the Sikh Foundation of Canada Inc. for having made this publication possible.

Seema Bharadia is an assistant curator in the Royal Ontario Museum.

Cover Image:

Maharaja Ranjit Singh with Emperor Akbar Shah II
1842
by William Parkinson
Lahore or Delhi
Drawing
Watercolour on paper
Suresh Bhalla Collection (Ontario)

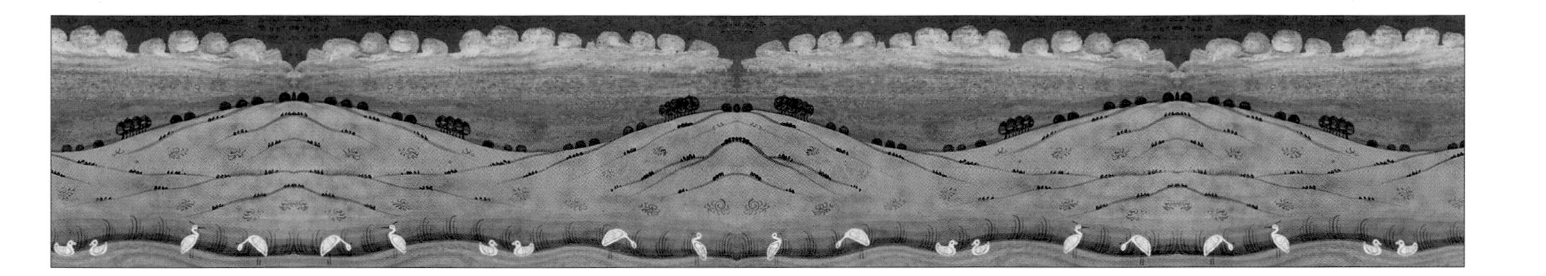

In the spring of 1999, *The Arts of the Sikh Kingdoms* transformed the appearance of the Victoria and Albert Museum. Sikh visitors arrived by the coach-load from all over the United Kingdom to see the exhibition, and the sounds of *bhangra* — traditional Sikh dance — echoed across the Victorian Italianate setting of the museum garden. Sparks flew — literally — as *gatka* practitioners demonstrated their extraordinary skill in this martial art to capacity audiences in the lecture theatre. Many of our visitors already knew the museum well, but many others came for the first time ever, especially to see this unique exhibition and to take part in the events associated with it. Most of the Sikhs were instantly identifiable because they wear the emblems of their religion adopted three centuries ago when Guru Gobind Singh initiated the *Khalsa*, the 300th anniversary of which the exhibition was celebrating.

Throughout the exhibition, and even before it began, enormous help and support from the Sikh community contributed significantly to its success. During the entire run, for example, a volunteer network of young men and women acted as interpreters, welcoming and guiding non-English speaking Punjabi visitors around the exhibition. The volunteers proved to be so friendly, approachable, and knowledgeable, that their assistance was sought equally by non-Sikhs, and they were able to answer all kinds of questions spontaneously put to them by a wide range of visitors about the general background to Sikh history and religion. Guides and visitors could constantly be seen in animated discussions around the Golden Throne of Maharaja Ranjit Singh, or in front of the vibrant paintings by a Lahore artist for one of the Maharaja's French generals.

When *The Arts of the Sikh Kingdoms* closed in London, the core of the exhibition travelled to San Francisco and then to Toronto, where it has acquired a new identity with the addition of more than forty objects from Canadian collections. This catalogue documents the artifacts unique to the exhibition in Toronto and, together with the sumptuous volume published by the Victoria and Albert Museum for the initial exhibition, provides a permanent record of the final incarnation of *The Arts of the Sikh Kingdoms*. With its showing of the exhibition in the spring and summer of 2000, the Royal Ontario Museum joins in the worldwide celebrations of the 300th anniversary of that transforming event in Sikh history, the founding of the *Khalsa*.

Susan Stronge
Curator, *The Arts of the Sikh Kingdoms*
Victoria and Albert Museum, London

The Royal Ontario Museum is pleased to host *The Arts of the Sikh Kingdoms*, an exhibition that celebrates the 300th anniversary of a pivotal event in Sikh history — the founding of the *Khalsa*, or "Fellowship of the Pure." The Victoria and Albert Museum, London, created the exhibition, which has had successful showings in London and at the Asian Art Museum, San Francisco. For the Toronto showing the exhibition has been complemented by a number of additional paintings, books, textiles, and other artifacts from the public collections, including loans, of the Royal Ontario Museum and the private collections of Sikh Canadians.

The Royal Ontario Museum wishes to thank the Sikh Canadian community for its generosity and assistance with the Toronto showing of *The Arts of the Sikh Kingdoms*. In particular, Lally Marwah has been of invaluable assistance with researching available Sikh-Canadian private collections for the supplementary objects to the original exhibition, and was the impetus for a permanent record of this collection in the form of a supplementary catalogue. In addition, the ROM acknowledges with gratitude the tireless efforts of T. Sher Singh, Suresh Bhalla, and the Sikh Foundation of Canada Inc. in assisting with the preparation of this catalogue. A special thanks to the following for generously lending objects from their private collections:

Suresh Bhalla (Ontario)

Baljit and Roshi Chadha (Quebec)

Harry Mann (Ontario)

Kanwar and Gurbachan Marwah (Ontario)

Lally and Marlène Marwah (Ontario)

Sabi and Amrin Marwah (Ontario)

Private Collection (British Columbia)

Ishar Singh/Mahinder Kaur Foundation (Ontario)

The ten Gurus with Mardana and Bala
c. 1800, Una, North India, gouache on paper
Lally and Marlène Marwah Collection (Ontario)

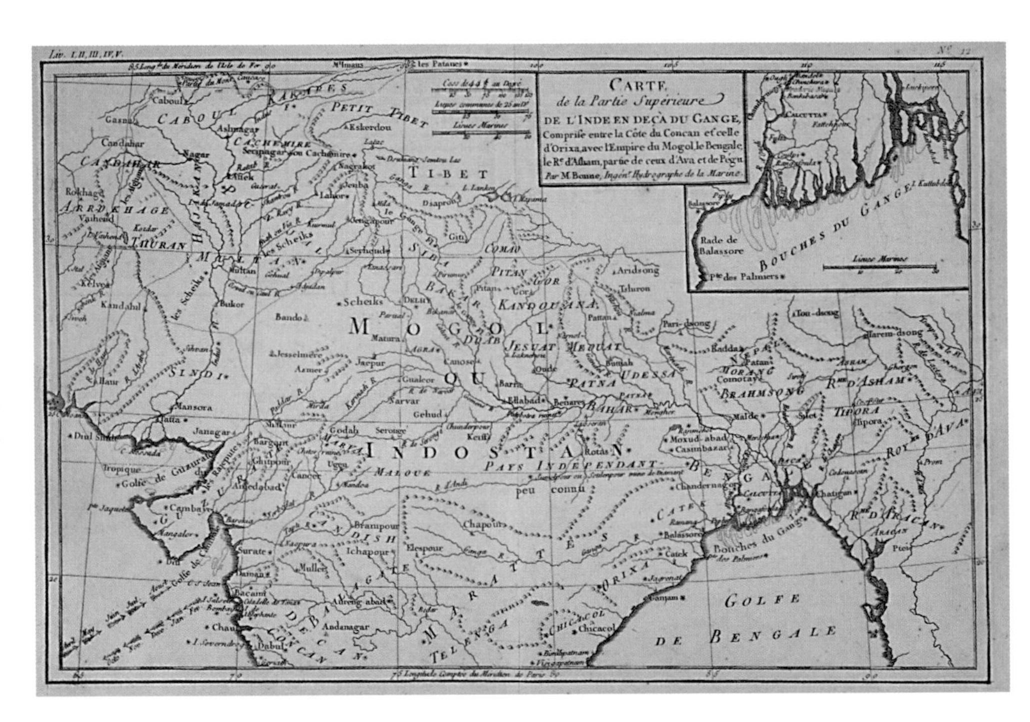

Early French map of the Punjab
c. 1780
by Rigobert Bonne
Paris, France
Ink on paper

This map was drawn by the cartographer Rigobert Bonne who was in the Punjab region in 1780. The labels "Les Scheiks" inscribed in the northwest identify the areas in which the Sikhs were predominant.

Lally and Marlène Marwah
Collection
(Ontario)

Sikhism began 500 years ago in the Punjab. This area of northwest India is rich and fertile, yet experiences the harshest of nature's extremes. Its seasons vary from exceptionally hot and dry, to the relief of monsoons, to freezing cold. In its peace and turbulence, nature reflects the history of this region.

Nanak, the founder of the Sikh faith, was born in 1469 in the village of Talvandi. In this small region, while the Punjab was experiencing Mughal invasions from the west, Hindus, Muslims, Buddhists, and Jains interacted with relative ease. The similarities and the differences between these faiths, in particular Hinduism and Islam, was a major influence on the already devoutly spiritual young

Guru Nanak, Mardana, and Bala
Early 1700s
Illumination from a *pothi*
Gouache and ink on paper

Pictures of Guru Nanak (1507–1539) usually show him in the company of his Hindu attendant, Bala, who holds a fly whisk, and his Muslim minstrel, Mardana, who carries a *rebec*.

Lally and Marlène Marwah Collection (Ontario)

Nanak. In addition to his native tongue, Punjabi, he learned to speak in the vernacular, as well as Sanskrit, Arabic, and Persian, in order to study the religious texts of the various faiths. Married at a young age, Nanak believed strongly in balancing spirituality with family life, and in the importance and equality of women in society. He approached his spiritual calling without discrimination or judgment of others. These experiences and beliefs sowed the seeds of a revolutionary philosophy of life and society in the Punjab, which came to be known as Sikhism.

The reappearance of Guru Nanak
1800s
Illustration
from a *Janam Sakhi* manuscript
Gouache on paper

Guru Nanak, still a young man, disappears while bathing in the Kali Bein, a tributary of River Beas. He reappears three days later, aglow with spiritual enlightenment, and proclaims his vision of a Universal Being by declaring, "There is no Hindu, there is no Musselman."

Sabi and Amrin Marwah
Collection
(Ontario)

A defining moment early in the adult life of Nanak marks the birth of Sikhism. Nanak disappeared for three days, during which time he experienced a revelation. Nanak realized that the various concepts of God in differing faiths all referred to One Universal Being, and that therefore in God's eyes all people are considered equal, regardless of caste, creed, or gender. Upon his reappearance, Nanak maintained a day of silence, after which he proclaimed the vital saying that became the starting point for his teachings:

There is no Hindu, nor Musselman [Muslim].

From this moment, Nanak dedicated his life to the teaching of this philosophy and came to be known as *Guru* or teacher. His disciples were called *Sikhs*, a term that evolved from the word *shishya*, meaning "disciple"or "pupil." Guru Nanak taught the existence of only One God, or *Ikk Oan Kar,* who is eternal and undefinable, who created all beings equally, and who on earth is manifested through His name *(Nam)*. This teaching is proclaimed at the start of the sacred *Jap Ji,* which is essentially a "key to the Sikh scripture" and contains the fundamental ideology of the Sikh faith. It is read and recited daily by Sikhs.

There is One Being
Truth by Name
Proclaimed Creator . . .

Truth before time
Truth throughout time

Says Nanak,
Truth is evermore.

Guru Nanak's teaching on ritual
1800s
Illustration
from a *Janam Sakhi* manuscript
Gouache on paper

Guru Nanak joins worshippers in the River Ganges at Hardwar, Uttar Pradesh. They are making water offerings to the sun. When Guru Nanak begins to scoop water in the opposite direction, the others ask what he is doing. He replies that if the water offered by the sun-worshippers can reach the sun, then perhaps water directed towards Punjab will reach his fields. In this way, he demonstrates his break from ritualistic worship.

Sabi and Amrin Marwah
Collection
(Ontario)

Guru Nanak and Nawab Daulat Khan
1800s
Illustration
from a *Janam Sakhi* manuscript
Gouache on paper

Guru Nanak is in discourse with his employer, Nawab Daulat Khan of Sultanpur Lodhi. Here, he emphasizes that all faiths are merely different paths to the same God who is the One God of all creation.

Sabi and Amrin Marwah
Collection
(Ontario)

Janam Sakhi
1777
Leather, gouache,
and gold on paper

Kanwar and Gurbachan Marwah
Collection
(Ontario)

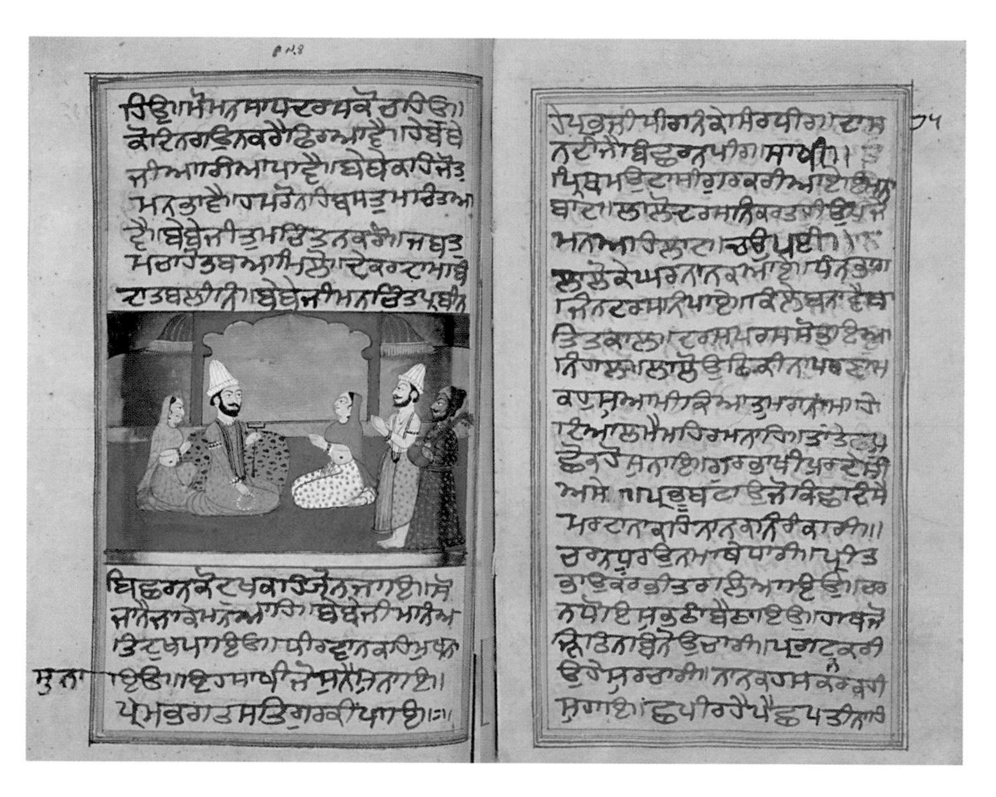

Janam Sakhi
1777
Leather, gouache,
and gold on paper

This rare manuscript is beautifully illuminated with the stories of Guru Nanak's life and travels. In this charming illustration Guru Nanak becomes lost in his poetry and songs of praise to God. Mardana, Bala, and a devotee appeal to the Guru's sister, Be-be Nanki, to encourage her brother to take some nourishment.

Kanwar and Gurbachan Marwah
Collection
(Ontario)

The life and travels of Guru Nanak have been chronicled in manuscripts known as *Janam Sakhis*. While the events recorded in these mauscripts are known to be factual, they were written after the death of the Guru, by his disciples and followers, and they are often told in the form of parables. *Janam Sakhis* are often illuminated with paintings that depict particular events in the Guru's life. Written in the beautiful *Gurmukhi* script, in Punjabi and other regional languages, *Janam Sakhis* are the first records in which Sikh subjects were represented through art.

Guru Nanak on the nature of Grace
1800s
Illustration
from a *Janam Sakhi* manuscript
Gouache on paper

Guru Nanak is speaking on the nature of Grace to Sheikh Ibrahim, who has arrived in a palanquin accompanied by Sheikh Kamal. The Guru is teaching that serving others is the greatest virtue and leads to a state of Grace.

Sabi and Amrin Marwah
Collection
(Ontario)

Guru Nanak and the courtesans of Kamrup, Assam
1800s
Illustration
from a *Janam Sakhi* manuscript
Gouache on paper

Guru Nanak resists the overtures of the courtesans of Kamrup while journeying to Assam in eastern India. His devoted minstrel, Mardana, enchanted by the seductive beauty of these women, is metaphorically depicted as a ram. Guru Nanak persuades the courtesans to live virtuous lives.

Sabi and Amrin Marwah
Collection
(Ontario)

Guru Nanak in the north country
1800s
Illustration
from a *Janam Sakhi* manuscript
Gouache on paper

Guru Nanak, Mardana, and a devotee prepare *rotis* or bread over a stone warmed by a hot-spring in the north country. This episode is thought to have occurred in Manipuran, in the Kulu Valley, where a *gurdwara* or Sikh temple stands today in commemoration of the Guru's visit.

Sabi and Amrin Marwah
Collection
(Ontario)

Guru Nanak and Emperor Babur
1800s
Illustration
from a *Janam Sakhi* manuscript
Gouache on paper

During a raid on the village of Saidpur, Guru Nanak and Mardana are briefly held captive by the army of Emperor Babur (1526–1530). Upon hearing of the Guru's reputation, the emperor receives Guru Nanak and Mardana at his court. Listening to the words of the Guru, Emperor Babur is humbled.

Sabi and Amrin Marwah
Collection
(Ontario)

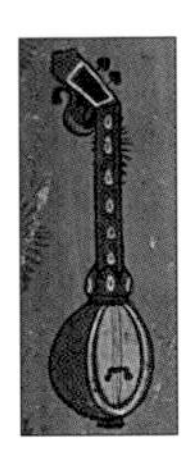

Guru Nanak and Guru Angad
1800s
Illustration
from a *Janam Sakhi* manuscript
Gouache on paper

Guru Nanak observes the deep faith and humility of his disciple Lehna, whom he chose as his successor, renaming him Guru Angad. The *Gurmukhi* script for the Punjabi language was invented by Guru Angad. The word *Gurmukhi* translates as "from the mouth of the Guru." *Gurmukhi* has remained the medium for sacred Sikh scriptures, and can be seen on *Janam Sakhis*, *pothis*, and the Sikh holy book, *Guru Granth Sahib*.

Sabi and Amrin Marwah
Collection
(Ontario)

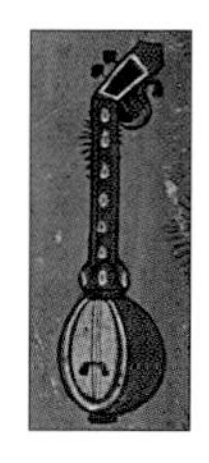

Pothi
Early 1700s
Ink on paper

Baljit and Roshi Chadha
Collection
(Quebec)

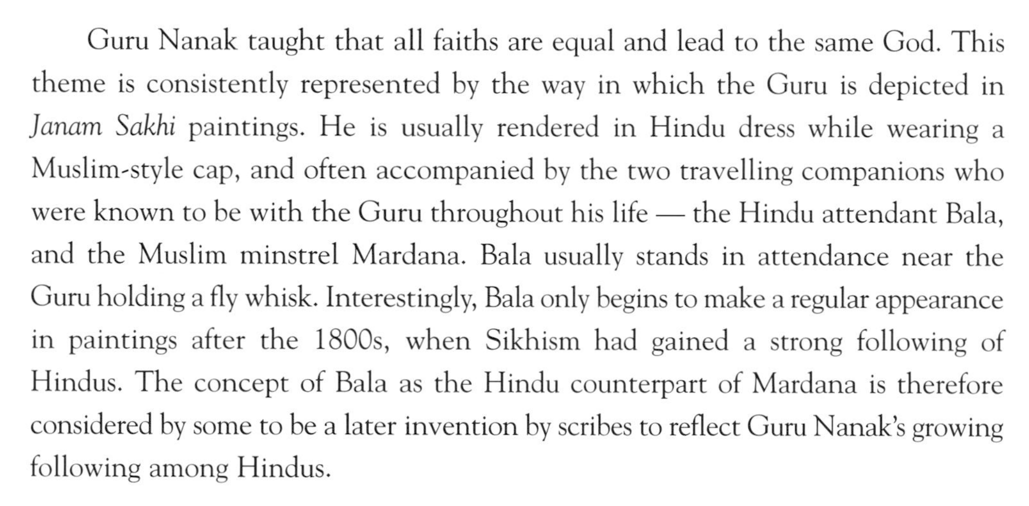

Guru Nanak taught that all faiths are equal and lead to the same God. This theme is consistently represented by the way in which the Guru is depicted in *Janam Sakhi* paintings. He is usually rendered in Hindu dress while wearing a Muslim-style cap, and often accompanied by the two travelling companions who were known to be with the Guru throughout his life — the Hindu attendant Bala, and the Muslim minstrel Mardana. Bala usually stands in attendance near the Guru holding a fly whisk. Interestingly, Bala only begins to make a regular appearance in paintings after the 1800s, when Sikhism had gained a strong following of Hindus. The concept of Bala as the Hindu counterpart of Mardana is therefore considered by some to be a later invention by scribes to reflect Guru Nanak's growing following among Hindus.

Guru Nanak, Mardana, and Bala
1700s
Frontispiece of a historic *Granth Sahib*
Gouache on paper

Lally and Marlène Marwah
Collection
(Ontario)

The ten Gurus
c. 1850
Gouache on paper

Suresh Bhalla
Collection
(Ontario)

Mardana the minstrel is well documented in early paintings as a constant companion of the Guru and is identified by his *rebec* or stringed instrument. When Guru Nanak recited his spiritual poetry, he was accompanied by Mardana on the *rebec*. The hymns sung today by Sikhs around the world have evolved from the compositions of Guru Nanak, which were originally recorded in manuscripts known as *pothis* (see p.23). Excerpts from *pothis* were eventually gathered in the Sikh sacred scripture known as the *Guru Granth Sahib*.

Before Guru Nanak died in 1539, he appointed a successor to carry on the spirit of his teachings. He chose his devout follower Lehna, and renamed him Guru Angad. *Ang* means "limb." By choosing this name for his successor Guru

The ten Gurus
Late 1800s/early 1900s
Oil on fabric

Harry Mann
Collection
(Ontario)

Nanak implied that Lehna was "of my own flesh." Thus began the tradition of successive Gurus, which carried on the teachings of Guru Nanak and established a strong faith and community. The succession of living gurus lasted for 200 years, ending with the tenth Guru, Gobind Singh, who passed the guruship to the sacred scripture *Guru Granth Sahib.*

There were no portraits painted of any of the Gurus during their lifetimes, but in the late 1700s and the 1800s the Gurus came to be represented by certain attributes that made them easily identifiable. For example, Guru Nanak is frequently depicted with a long white beard, wearing a Muslim cap and Hindu robes, and is often seen with his two disciples, Mardana and Bala. Guru Har Krishan is the only

Ten Gurus rumala
c. 1910
Possibly from Shanghai
Silk and brocade

This representation of the ten Gurus is particularly interesting in that the facial features of the Gurus, Mardana, and Bala are those of the Far East, evidencing the far-reaching influence of Guru Nanak's teachings. The maker of this beautiful embroidery may have been from Shanghai. This *rumala* would have been used to cover the *Guru Granth Sahib*.

Suresh Bhalla
Collection
(Ontario)

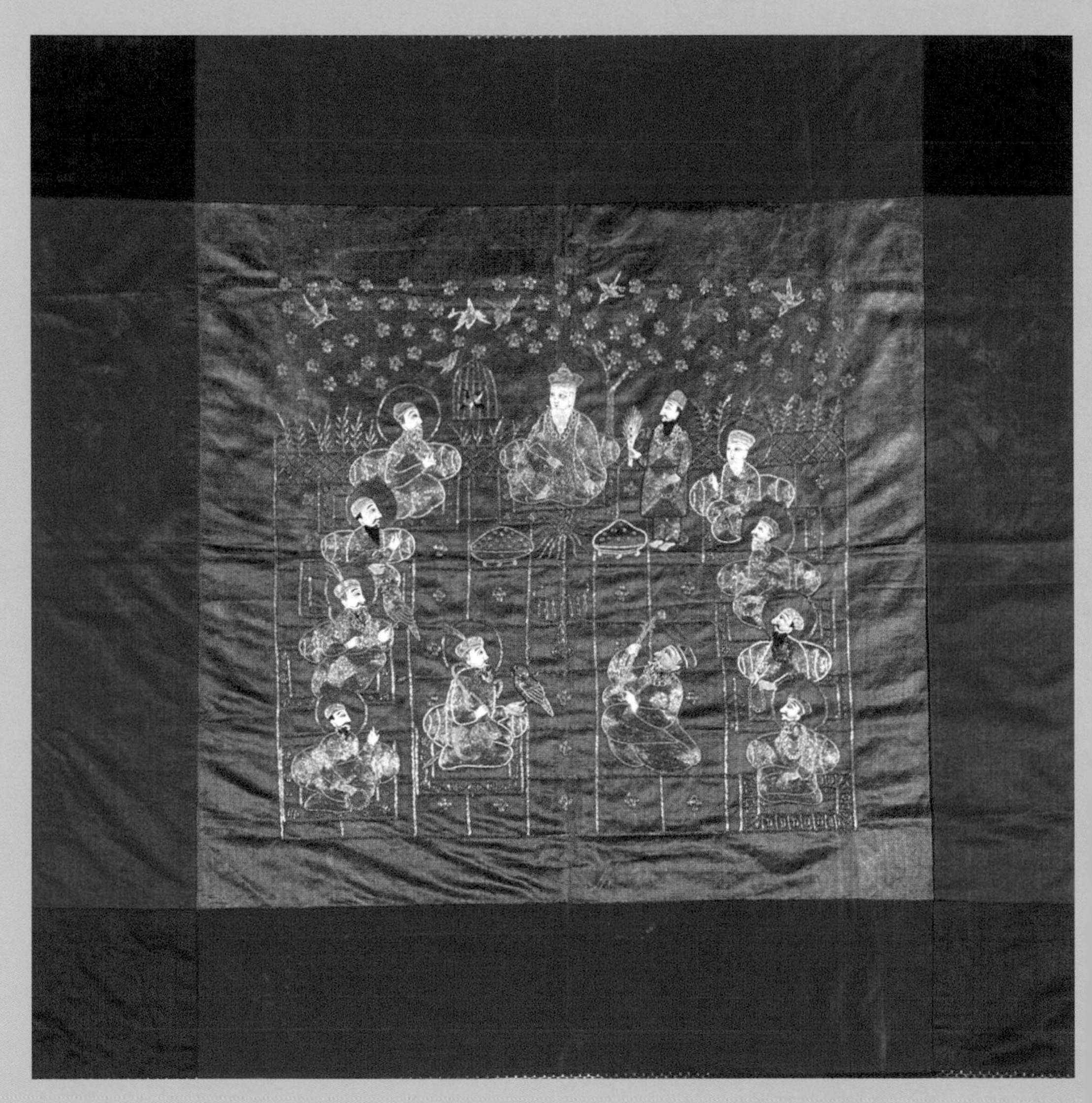

Guru seen without a beard, because he died before he reached adulthood. Guru Gobind Singh is usually shown as a majestic figure on horseback holding a falcon.

The depiction of all ten Gurus seated together in a circle with Mardana and Bala has become distinctively iconographic. A nimbus behind the head of each Guru symbolizes his spiritual and temporal sovereignty. This presentation captures the belief that the spirit of Guru Nanak continued from one Guru to the next for more than two centuries. The scene commemorates the culmination of the Gurus combined teachings.

The fourth Guru, Ram Das (1574–1581), founded the town of Amritsar. The site was originally selected by the second Guru, Angad (1539–1552). It was a calm pool surrounded by trees in the countryside. The third Guru, Amar Das (1552–1574), found it an ideal place for meditation, and Guru Ram Das foresaw it as the setting of a shrine that would be a monument to the Sikh faith. Guru Ram Das bought the land and began the excavation of the pool. Soon after, under the guruship of Arjan (1581–1606), the fifth Guru, construction began on the great Sikh monument known as the *Harmandir* and later as the Golden Temple. The foundation stone was laid in 1588. Artisans and traders were encouraged to settle in the town and contributed to its rapid growth. It quickly became one of the largest commercial centres in northern India.

Guru Amar Das (1552–1574)
Late 1800s
Gouache on paper

Guru Amar Das was a devout follower of Guru Angad, who chose him to be the third Guru in 1552. Amar Das was in his seventies at the time. He continued Nanak's teaching of gender equality by appointing three women as preachers.

Lally and Marlène Marwah
Collection
(Ontario)

Guru Amar Das (1552–1574)
Late 1800s
Gouache on paper

Paintings of the Sikh Gurus flourished predominantly in the 1800s, a century after the death of the last living Guru. The style of representation varies according to the imagination of each individual artist and the particular stories with which he grew up. Here, for instance, the artist has pictured Guru Amar Das as elderly and humble, and the neighbouring image of Guru Amar Das shows him with the same personality and posture but remarkably different physical characteristics.

Sabi and Amrin Marwah Collection (Ontario)

Golden Temple address casket
Late 1800s
Silver, silver gilt, ivory, cotton, brocade, wood, paint

This magnificent piece is an address casket in the shape of the Golden Temple or *Harmandir*. The front section pulls out into a drawer which is elaborately painted with Kashmiri floral designs. The interior is fully detailed with the intricate patterns of the temple itself.

Ornately decorated boxes such as this were made to hold manuscript scrolls or addresses proclaiming loyalty to the Crown. Many such address caskets were presented to Queen Victoria, particularly on special occasions such as her Golden and Diamond Jubilees. This model of the Golden Temple may have contained a loyal address for Queen Victoria or for her son Edward VII.

RCIN 59101

Golden Temple address casket
View from rear steps
Silver, silver gilt, ivory, cotton, brocade, wood, paint

The Golden Temple address casket was lent to the Royal Ontario Museum in 1939 together with other artifacts and has remained on extended loan since that time. The loan was organized by the Victoria and Albert Museum on behalf of the Royal Family.

Golden Temple plan
1900s
Gouache on fabric

This rendition of the Golden Temple site shows the buildings surrounding the *Harmandir* elevated from the floor plan itself. The details of the windows indicate the direction in which each building is oriented.

Harry Mann
Collection
(Ontario)

The *Harmandir* is a magnificent structure and became a major focal point for Sikhdom. It is the first and most important sacred building of the Sikh faith and a repository for the original sacred texts. Guru Arjan envisioned a shrine that would reflect the characteristics of the new Sikh faith. The building was to be set in the centre of a sacred pool of water, its location symbolizing the synthesis of *nirgun* and *sargun*, the spiritual and temporal realms of human existence. There are doorways on all four sides of the building to denote the acceptance of all people regardless of status or religious backround. To emphasize the concept of humility, the *Harmandir* was built at a level lower than the surrounding land, and slopes to an even lower level towards the back steps.

As the most visible and impressive symbol of the Sikh faith and community, the *Harmandir* has been the subject of repeated attack. It was damaged and rebuilt or restored several times. Under the stable government of Ranjit Singh (1801–1839), the *Harmandir* underwent a significant renovation. The Maharaja chose marble and gold as the primary materials for refurbishing and expansion. Marble panels were inlaid with intricate floral, natural, abstract, and geometric designs and motifs. Using a technique called *jaratkari*, semi-precious stones such as onyx, mother-of-pearl, lapis lazuli, and red carnelian were inlaid into the marble. Fresco painting called *dehin* adorned the inside of the temple. The interior sparkled with the reflections of *gach* — gold leaf applied to etched gypsum, and *tukri* — coloured and mirrored glass cut and inlaid into the *gach*.

Door details of the Golden Temple
1882–1883
by Adbul Aziz
Possibly Amritsar
Lithographs

These lithographs provide details of the wood and ivory panels on the *Darshani Darwaza,* or the doors of the Golden Temple. They were commissioned for the project named a "Preservation of National Monuments in India," by curator Major Cole, R. E., from the Ancient Monuments in India.

Suresh Bhalla
Collection
(Ontario)

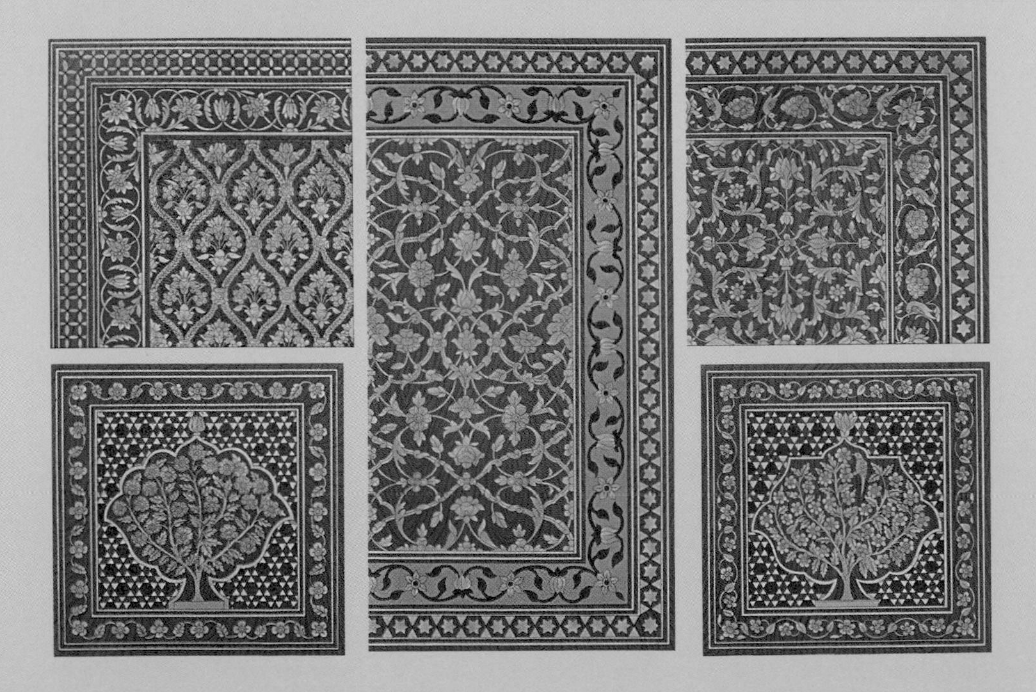

Door details of the Golden Temple
1882–1883
by Adbul Aziz
Possibly Amritsar
Lithographs

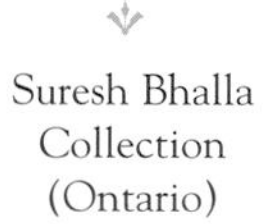

Suresh Bhalla
Collection
(Ontario)

The journey to sustain the Sikh faith was marked by Mughal persecution. The influence of the Gurus, their refusal to embrace Islam, and the growing strength of Sikhism provoked the hostility of the Mughal rulers. Two Sikh Gurus became martyrs to the cause of religious freedom. They were the fifth Guru, Arjan Dev, in 1606, and the ninth Guru, Tegh Bahadur, in 1675.

Guru Arjan was arrested and died as a result of torture ordered by the Mughal emperor Jahangir (1605–1628), who feared the Guru's influence. After Arjan's death, his son and successor, Guru Har Gobind (1606–1644), began to organize his followers into an armed force in order to protect the faith. At the same time measures were taken to protect the *Harmandir* by surrounding it with buildings, such as the Akal Takht, or "Throne of the Timeless [God]."

Door details of the Golden Temple
1882–1883
by Adbul Aziz
Possibly Amritsar
Lithographs

Suresh Bhalla
Collection
(Ontario)

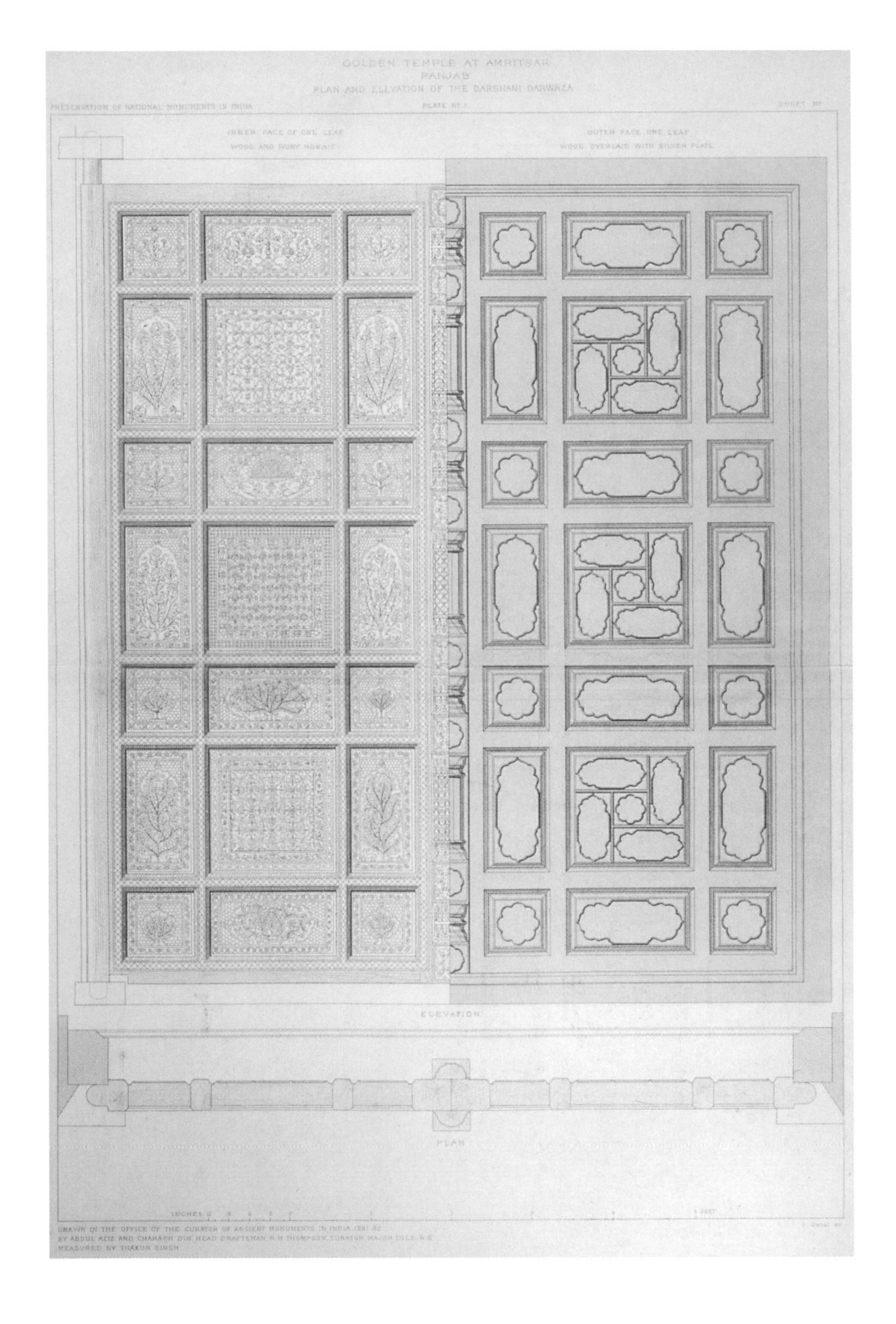

Carved door panel
undated
Sultanpur Lodhi
Wood

Design styles of Punjab were incorporated in many different media. The woodwork on this panel is typical of that found in the region during the 1600s and is reminiscent of design elements used in the Golden Temple.

Ishar Singh/Mahinder Kaur Foundation (Ontario)

The introduction and need for protection began to change the face of the Sikh community and can be understood in terms of the concept of *miri* and *piri*, symbolized by two swords and presented by Guru Har Gobind. *Piri* derives from the word *pir*, which in Sufism means a "religious teacher," and symbolizes spirituality; *miri* derives from the word *amir*, also from Islamic roots, which means "commander," and symbolizes the political power of the spiritual community. These two ideas came to be jointly represented by the *Khanda* — the image of two swords, one balancing the other — which has become emblematic of the Sikh community (see page 57).

The emphasis on spiritual and temporal responsibility continues to be central to Sikhism. The tradition of resisting oppression began with Guru Nanak and continued through to the tenth Guru, Gobind Singh (1675–1708). The Gurus were religious leaders, but they were also inevitably politically involved in Punjab through their need to protect their community from religious persecution.

Over time, the spiritual and political symbols of *piri* and *miri* have been transferred to *tegh* and *deg*, literally "the sword" and "the cooking pot." Figuratively, they refer to protecting the oppressed and feeding the hungry. Warfare and the use of the sword came to be considered the last resort to defend the community from tyranny, and to ensure its safety and survival.

Under the leadership of Guru Har Gobind, Sikhs began to develop a strong military community. Sixty-nine years after the death of Guru Arjan, however, Guru Tegh Bahadur (1664–1675) was sentenced to death by Emperor Aurangzeb for refusing to renounce his faith. Tegh Bahadur's nine-year-old son, Gobind Singh, succeeded him as Guru. Gobind Singh was to spend his life preparing for what would be one of the most significant moments in Sikh history and identity.

Guru Har Krishan (1661–1664)
1820
Gouache on paper

The eighth Guru, Har Krishan, is always depicted in paintings as a child. In 1661, at the age of five, he was nominated successor to his father, Guru Har Rai (1630–1661). In 1664 Guru Har Krishan was summoned by Emperor Aurangzeb (1658–1707) to the Mughal court, where he tragically died of smallpox at the age of eight. The Guruship then passed to Guru Tegh Bahadur (1664–1675).

Private Collection
(British Columbia)

Guru Gobind Singh
1820
Gouache on paper

This early portrait of Guru Gobind Singh shows him seated in a terrace with two attendants. He carries the symbols by which he has come to be identified, the bow and arrow, sword, and shield. After the establishment of the *Khalsa* (1699), he was typically shown riding a horse.

Private Collection
(British Columbia)

Guru Gobind Singh (1675–1708) was the last of the ten Gurus. He decreed that with his death the line of succession by living Gurus would end. The Sikh holy book, *Guru Granth Sahib*, was proclaimed as the permanent Guru. It comprises the collected teachings of the previous Sikh Gurus, with compositions by mystics and saints from a number of other religious traditions. It was initially compiled and placed with reverence in the *Harmandir* by the fifth Guru, Arjan, in 1604.

In 1699, Guru Gobind Singh established the *Khalsa* or "Fellowship of the Pure." He chose the five founding members of the *Khalsa* by means of a test to determine the strength of their commitment to the faith. The founding was solemnized in a ceremony of initiation which included sipping *amrit* (sweetened water) stirred with a double-edged sword, symbolizing the One Universal God.

Guru Gobind Singh sought to eliminate caste distinctions inherent in one's surname, by encouraging all men to take the same surname, Singh, meaning "lion," and all women to take the same surname, Kaur, meaning "princess" or "lioness." Additionally, he initiated the adoption of the "Five Ks" or five articles of faith, both spiritual and martial, by which Sikhs have generally come to be identified.

The "Five Ks"

Kesh:	Uncut hair symbolizes saintliness, holiness, and one's commitment to spirituality. The long hair of men is held neatly in place with the turban.
Kanga:	The comb is necessary to keep the hair groomed, and signifies cleanliness.
Kara:	The steel bangle worn on the wrist. Its circular shape symbolizes God who has no beginning and no end; it also symbolizes self discipline and a commitment to serving society.
Kaccha:	Short breeches signify a chaste and dignified code of conduct.
Kirpan:	The short, ceremonial sword symbolizes one's commitment to serve the community at large by upholding justice. It is also a symbol of courage, dignity, protection, and self-reliance.

Guru Gobind Singh urged his followers "to uphold right in every place . . . that right may triumph, [and] good may live," and taught that "when all other means have failed, it is righteous to draw the sword." Through this teaching and the incorporation of the *Khalsa,* the Sikh community developed a cohesive identity in the Punjab. Following a series of nine Afghan invasions from 1748 to 1768, the Sikhs became organized into a confederacy of twelve separate commands or *misls* spread throughout the Punjab. Within a hundred years of the establishment of the *Khalsa* the Sikhs had become a formidable military force.

Maharaja Ranjit Singh with Emperor Akbar Shah II
1842
by William Parkinson
Lahore or Delhi
Drawing
Watercolour on paper

European artists were enamoured of the Sikh court. This painting by British artist William Parkinson shows Maharaja Ranjit Singh (r. 1801–1839) meeting the Mughal emperor Akbar II for the signing of treaties. The subject demonstrates the importance of Ranjit Singh in the imagination of Europeans even after his death in 1839.

Suresh Bhalla
Collection
(Ontario)

Maharaja Ranjit Singh (1780–1839)
Mid-1800s
From a series of fourteen ivories
Watercolour on ivory

Maharaja Ranjit Singh (r. 1801–1839) would rarely concede to the painting of his portrait because he was blind in one eye and disfigured from a childhood experience of smallpox. For the same reasons he is clearly distinguishable in court paintings and portraiture.

Sabi and Amrin Marwah Collection (Ontario)

The military and political strength of the Sikhs culminated in the emergence of a strong leader, the young warrior Ranjit Singh, who through marriage combined two of the most powerful *misls* into one force. In 1799 at the head of his *Khalsa* armies, he captured the Mughal city of Lahore, and in 1801 proclaimed himself maharaja of Punjab. Eventually he acquired military technology modelled upon that of Europe, and numbers of Europeans, including generals from Napoleon's armies, would join his Sikh forces. Ranjit Singh's authority began in the plains of northern India and in time stretched to the Punjab Hills, as far west as Afghanistan and as far northeast as Ladakh. During Ranjit Singh's reign (1801–1839), the Punjab knew relatively peaceful times in which both the economy and the arts flourished.

Emperor Bahadur Shah II
c. 1850
Gouache on paper

Bahadur Shah II (r. 1837–1857), the last of the Mughal emperors, was also a poet, and is seen here with writing tools. He is seated on a replica of the Peacock Throne, originally built by Shah Jahan (r. 1628–1658). Bahadur Shah lived his final years in exile in Burma as a result of his involvement the Indian Mutiny of 1857.

Royal Ontario Museum
927.86.2

A Mughal coronation scene with Maharaja Ranjit Singh
Mid-1800s
Watercolour on ivory

The Mughal emperors had governed the Punjab region for over 250 years when Ranjit Singh came to power in Punjab in 1801. This painting on ivory shows the last Mughal emperor, Bahadur Shah II (1837–1857), at top and centre. Ranjit Singh can be seen on the right with Gulab Singh at the left, and possibly his son Kharak Singh at the bottom. The portraits of women may be the wives of these leaders of northern India.

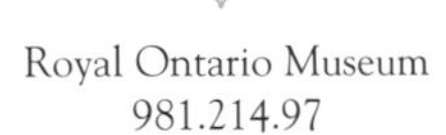

Royal Ontario Museum
981.214.97

Maharaja Ranjit Singh was an enormous patron of the arts, and under his able and peaceful rule the arts developed and prospered. His court or *durbar* included individuals from a variety of traditions and knew no religious boundaries. Beautiful and lasting works of art created during the reign of Ranjit Singh, by Muslim, Hindu, and Sikh artists, ranged from miniature paintings of the Pahari Hills, to intricately woven multi-coloured shawls and carpets, and included metalwork and ceramics. The maharaja ordered the restoration of the *Harmandir* and covered its turrets in gold; thus it has come to be known as the Golden Temple.

Maharaja Ranjit Singh and Sikh noblemen
Mid-1800s
Series of fourteen ivories
Watercolour on ivory

Ranjit Singh's court or *durbar* consisted of his sons and other noblemen. These intricately painted ivories serve as records of individuals involved in the court politics of Punjab in the1800s.

Sabi and Amrin Marwah Collection (Ontario)

Sikh coins
c. 1800s
Punjab, Amritsar, and Lahore
Silver, copper, and silver alloy

Maharaja Ranjit Singh (r. 1801–1839) introduced a new currency under his reign. Breaking from the previous tradition of issuing currency in the name of the ruler, the maharaja issued coins with the names of Guru Nanak and Guru Gobind Singh. They were inscribed with couplets called *Nanakshahi* and *Gobindshahi*. The silver rupee and *mohur* used Persian for their primary script, while local languages of northwest India were used for copper coins.

Ishar Singh/Mahinder Kaur Foundation (Ontario)

The opulence of the court of Maharaja Ranjit Singh was in direct contrast to the man himself. When guests, particularly foreign visitors, were present, the maharaja occupied his Golden Throne, and his court was resplendent with richly patterned, vibrantly coloured carpets and textiles. In private, however, he was a quiet man of modesty, and could often be seen seated on a simple chair in humble surroundings.

As the balance of power in Punjab shifted from the Mughals to the Sikhs, the famed jewels known as the Koh-i-nur diamond and the "Timur Ruby" also passed to the Sikh maharaja. Ranjit Singh's son Sher Singh was painted posthumously wearing both these jewels in 1850. Other treasures of the court included wooden cabinets beautifully inlaid with ivory and tortoise shell, ornately decorated jade

Maharaja Kharak Singh
Mid-1800s
From a series of fourteen ivories
Watercolour on ivory

Kharak Singh, the eldest son of Ranjit Singh, succeeded his father as maharaja in 1839 but ruled for only a year before he died.

Sabi and Amrin Marwah Collection (Ontario)

objects and ceremonial weapons, and jewels and medals encrusted with emeralds and diamonds. Today the Koh-i-nur diamond and the "Timur Ruby" are in the holdings of the Royal Collections of Her Majesty Queen Elizabeth II.

Ranjit Singh's shrewdness and cosmopolitan nature, combined with his great strength of character, brought him immense respect and earned him the title "Lion of Punjab." He was a skilled leader who was able to maintain stability and keep foreign powers at bay throughout his reign.

Maharaja Sher Singh
Mid 1800s
Paint on ivory

Sher Singh was a son of Ranjit Singh. His short rule of the Punjab lasted only three years, from 1840 to 1843.

Royal Ontario Museum
981.214.135

After the death of Maharaja Ranjit Singh in 1839 the Punjab fell into turmoil. His son Kharak Singh, who succeeded him as ruler of Punjab, died within a year and is believed to have been murdered. Ranjit Singh's son Sher Singh ascended the throne next but was murdered in 1843 as a result of political dissension aggravated by the British presence in the Punjab. The next in the line of succession was Ranjit Singh's youngest son, Dalip Singh, a five-year-old child. Internal rivalries weakened the Punjab and led to further encroachment by the British. Following the Anglo-Sikh wars of 1845–46 and 1848–49, and ten years after the death of Maharaja Ranjit Singh, Britain gained final rule of the Punjab, thereby completing its conquest of India.

When the British gained administrative control of the region, they confirmed Dalip Singh as maharaja and made him a ward of Queen Victoria. After the first Anglo-Sikh war, but before Punjab's annexation, however, the British separated the ten-year-old Dalip Singh from his mother, Rani Jindan Kaur. The young maharaja was placed in the care of John Login, a Scottish doctor living in India. Isolated from his family and separated from his cultural roots, Dalip Singh was raised in the Christian tradition. In 1854 at the age of fifteen he was taken to England, where he became a favourite of Queen Victoria and a playmate for her children.

Rani Jindan Kaur with her son, Maharaja Dalip Singh
1840
Lahore
Watercolour on paper

This painting is thought to be of Rani Jindan Kaur and her son, Dalip Singh. Rani Jindan Kaur was born to a peasant family in a small village in the district of Gujranwala. She was twenty-two years old when she became the widow of Maharaja Ranjit Singh. Her son was proclaimed maharaja in 1843 and she acted as regent during the early part of his reign.

Suresh Bhalla
Collection
(Ontario)

Rani Jindan Kaur, meanwhile, lived a life of exile in Nepal. In 1859 Dalip Singh travelled to Bombay where he was reunited with his mother. They returned together to his home in England, but shortly afterwards, in 1863, Rani Jindan died at the age of forty-six. Dalip Singh married Bamba Muller in 1864 and they had several children. He reverted to the Sikh faith in 1886 and spent the remainder of his life strengthening his Sikh identity and attempting, unsuccessfully, to reinstate his claim to the Punjab. He died of a stroke in Paris in 1893.

After the turbulence of the establishment of the British Raj, there was a renaissance of the arts in Punjab. While the new European patrons provided a platform for artists to create tourist and trade items, the legendary splendours of Maharaja Ranjit Singh's court continued to inspire the artists of the Punjab in the latter part of the 1800s. *Pashmina* shawls and *phulkari* embroideries were produced and traded. Portraits of prominent individuals flourished once more, and paintings began to depict the daily life and events of the Sikh community. The tradition of carved inlaid wood and marble returned and metalworkers continued to produce their intricate creations. The remarkable contributions of these artists in turn continue to inspire artists of the present day.

Sikhs in Canada

The first Sikhs recorded as having visited Canada were members of the Punjabi regiment of Hong Kong, who accompanied the 1897 celebration of Queen Victoria's Diamond Jubilee. Drawn to the opportunities, climate, and environment of British Columbia — similar to their own homeland of Punjab — many Sikh men began to make arrangements to travel and explore the possibilities of Canada as a new home. The journey from India began with a train ride to Calcutta, followed by a boat trip to Hong Kong, where, after a long wait, they began the final sea voyage to Canada.

Between 1904 and 1908, approximately 5000 Sikh men settled in British Columbia, working in the lumber, railway, and forestry industries. The next decade, however, saw a struggle to gain governmental support for more Sikhs and their families to enter the country. In 1914, more than 350 Indians, predominantly Sikhs, arrived at Burrard Inlet on the ship *Komagata Maru,* but were denied entry and had to return home. In 1915, the first Sikh arrived in Ontario from British Columbia to lobby for the entry of Sikh women and children into Canada, which was eventually permitted in 1919.

BHAI GURDIT SINGH AND THE PARTY OF 375 HINDUSTANEES ON BOARD S. S. KOMAGATA MARU

Sikh Canadians were granted the vote and became full citizens of the country in 1947. During the second half of the 20th century, more than a quarter of a million Sikhs from around the world made Canada their home. They arrived from South Asia, England, East Africa, New Zealand, Afghanistan, and Southeast Asia. Building on the successes of their forefathers, today's Sikh Canadians continue to maintain their cultural and religious identity, while significantly contributing to Canada as entrepreneurs, politicians, farmers, entertainers, scholars, athletes, artists, and professionals.

Sikh Canadian Centennial stamp
1997
designed by Stacey Zabolotney

In 1997, when Canada's Sikh community celebrated the 100th anniversary of the first settlement of Sikhs in Canada, the Government of Canada issued a commemorative stamp. The stamp, which features the Sikh emblem known as the *Khanda*, honours the contributions of Sikhs in Canada over the last century.

The Arts of the Sikh Kingdoms
Royal Ontario Museum
Exhibition Poster
designed by Teikna Graphics Inc.

References

Arayan, K. C. *Punjab Painting*. Patiala: Punjabi University, 1977.

Brown, Kerry, ed. *Sikh Art and Literature*. London and New York: Routledge, 1999.

Cole, W. Owen, and Piara Singh Sambhi. *The Sikhs: Their Religious Beliefs and Practices*. London and Boston: Routledge and Kegan Paul, 1978.

Goswamy, B. N. *Piety and Splendor: Sikh Hertiage in Art*. New Delhi: National Museum, 2000.

Jagpal, Sarjeet Singh. *Becoming Canadians: Pioneer Sikhs in Their Own Words*. Madeira Park and Vancouver: Harbour Publishing, 1994.

McLeod, W. H. *Popular Sikh Art*. Oxford: Oxford University Press, 1991.

McLeod, W. H. *Guru Nanak and the Sikh Religion*. Oxford: Clarendon Press, 1968.

Singh, Khushwant, and Raghu Rai. *The Sikhs*. Calcutta: Lustre Press Pvt Ltd., 1984.

Singh, Patwant. *The Sikhs*. London: John Murray, 1999.

Singh, Patwant. *The Golden Temple*. Hong Kong: ET Publishing Ltd., 1988.

Singh, T. Sher, ed. *The Century in Canada 1897–1997: The Promise and the Challenge*. Guelph: The Centennial Foundation, 1997.

Stronge, Susan, ed. *The Arts of the Sikh Kingdoms*. London: V&A Publications, 1999.

Photograph Credits

Sarjeet Singh Jagpal (Archival)
Gurbachan Kaur Marwah (End pages)
Lally and Marlène Marwah (Archival)

Exhibition Sponsor

Honorary Patron

Harbanse (Herb) Doman

Exhibition Patrons

Cedara Software Corp
Eglinton Carpet Corp.
HSBC Bank Canada
Scotia Bank
Suresh and Nutan Bhalla
Chadha Family Foundation
Dr. and Mrs. Jatinder S. Dhillon
Purewal Blueberry Farms (Vancouver)
Mata Kishan Kaur Sidhu (in memory)

The Arts of the Sikh Kingdoms is organized by the Victoria and Albert Museum, London. It is presented by the ROM with the support of the Sikh Foundation of Canada Inc.

The support of the Government of Ontario, through Ontario 2000 and the Ministry of Citizenship, Culture and Recreation, is gratefully acknowledged.

Financial support has been provided by the Department of Canadian Heritage.